MW01618116

panini

RECIPES Melanie Barnard
PHOTOGRAPHS Lara Hata

A Fireside Book
Published by Simon & Schuster
New York London Toronto Sydney

contents

hot off the press

Panini, the traditional Italian grilled sandwiches, have become increasingly popular in recent years. Originally filled with only sliced meats and cheeses, these delicious preparations can now be found stuffed and grilled with any number of ingredients to suit the occasion. Whether you're preparing a casual lunch, a creative dinner, or a sweet treat, panini are a creative palette on which to present the best seasonal produce, high-quality meats, and a variety of sauces and spreads. Simply assemble your creation, grill, and serve!

use the best ingredients

In Italian, the word *panino* refers to both "sandwich" and "bread roll," but the term is most often used to describe a sandwich that has been grilled. Traditionally, panini are two slices of lightly oiled bread filled with a combination of sliced meats and cheeses. The bread is then pressed and grilled, yielding a hot sandwich with grill-marked bread and melted cheese. However, pairing a little creativity with a variety of good-quality ingredients, panini can also be stuffed with fruit, vegetables, and flavorful spreads or toppings.

There is more to panini, however, than the grilling. It's important to think about the kind of bread used in addition to the fillings in between the slices. You'll notice a wide variety of breads used throughout the recipes in this book. Country-style bread is a good choice for panini because it is sturdy, firm textured, and pairs well with a variety of ingredients. But when panini are inspired by traditional recipes such as The Reuben (page 66), a Southwestern Chicken Quesadilla (page 40), or sweet Strawberry Shortcakes (page 77) the ingredients fill the corresponding bread; rye for the corned beef, flour tortillas for the chicken and cheese, and fresh shortcakes for the strawberries.

When it comes to fillings, try different combinations of your favorite sliced meats and cheeses, or enjoy the range of traditional and contemporary recipes presented throughout this book. The glossary on pages 90–91 will introduce you to some of the many different cheeses, meats, vegetables, fruits, and garnishes that can be used to make panini. To make the most of fresh, local produce, visit a nearby farmers' market or see the chart on the following page for a list of the fruits, vegetables, and fresh herbs that thrive in each season.

think seasonally

Use the guidelines below to choose the best fresh produce that each season has to offer.

spring try asparagus, fresh herbs (such as cilantro, dill, chives, parsley, and mint), green onions, and strawberries.

summer make the most of arugula leaves, bell peppers, corn, cucumbers, fresh herbs (such as parsley, basil, and thyme), tomatoes, and zucchini as well as peaches, nectarines, and raspberries.

autumn fall's best produce includes a variety of wild and cultivated mushrooms, fresh herbs (such as rosemary and sage), along with apples, nuts, and pears.

winter enjoy fresh herbs (such as rosemary and sage), turnip greens, wild and cultivated mushrooms, apples, pears, citrus fruits, and pineapple.

turn your panini into a meal

Whether you are serving panini for a creative after-school snack, a weekend brunch, or a casual dinner with guests, enhance your meal with a fresh green salad, a bowl of soup, a handful of Homemade Potato Chips (page 88), or Sweet Potato Wedges (page 88). Choose side dishes that complement the flavors in your panini: Serve a cucumber salad with a Mediterranean sandwich or corn chips and Fresh Tomato Salsa (page 89) with a Mexican-themed preparation. Explore the suggestions on pages 88–89 for more inspiration.

If you like, choose an appropriate beverage that works well with your panini. For a light summer lunch, serve Curried Chicken Salad panini (page 39) with a pitcher of iced tea or fresh lemonade. PB & J panini (page 28) are a great snack, perfect for people of all ages with a tall glass of cold milk. Cinnamon-Apple Stuffed Pancakes (page 81) make a terrific breakfast panini and can be served with a steaming cup of French roast coffee or fresh-squeezed orange juice.

If you have unexpected company, panini are a quick and creative meal option. Consider serving a cold artisan pale ale to complement Rustic Turkey with Brie & Apples (page 33) or a glass of dry white Spanish wine to balance the bold flavors of the Spicy Tuna Bocadillo (page 51). The Honey-Drizzled Pears with Gorgonzola & Walnuts (page 83) are enhanced with Sambuca, an anise liqueur; serve this exotic treat after dinner, accompanied by a small glass of the same liqueur on the side.

panini equipment and grilling tips

Some sandwich grills are made specifically to grill panini, and they can often grill two sandwiches at once, a boon when you are serving several people. This piece of equipment is a good investment if you plan to make a lot of panini. Be sure to read the manufacturer's instructions to learn how your sandwich grill should be operated and cleaned. Heavy stovetop pans with ridged bottoms can be used to make panini, too. Some come with a weighted press, but you can press down firmly on the sandwich with a metal spatula, if needed.

Have a metal spatula on hand to remove finished panini from the sandwich grill. This will help ensure that the ingredients don't fall out of the sandwich and that the bread stays in one piece. You can use nonstick cooking spray on the sandwich grill before grilling the sandwiches so the finished panini are easier to remove.

It is helpful to have all of the ingredients ready before you assemble and grill panini. Read the recipe before you begin to see if any ingredients need to be cooked in advance; keep in mind that poultry, meats, fish, and produce can often be cooked on the sandwich grill. This will save you time and make cleanup easier, and it also adds flavor to the sandwiches. Often, foods cooked on the sandwich grill will leave behind a char that flavors the bread when it is grilled. Whenever possible in these recipes, instructions for cooking fillings on the sandwich grill are included.

Once you have assembled the panini, be sure the sandwich grill is hot enough before you use it. As you become familiar with your sandwich grill, you will know how it indicates that the correct temperature has been reached. (Many sandwich grills have an indicator light.) During cooking, stay near the sandwich grill and lift the plate occasionally to check for doneness.

Try not to pack too many ingredients into a single panino. Once it is closed, the weight of the sandwich grill will sometimes cause some of the fillings to fall out, where they can make cleanup more difficult. However, don't be concerned if there is a little cheese oozing onto the bread crust or pieces of the filling coming out of the side; these details are part of what make panini so enjoyable to eat.

Finally, have ready appropriate serving platters or dishes and eating utensils. Some panini are open-faced and best served with a knife and fork. Others can be enjoyed out of hand like traditional sandwiches. Serving suggestions and ideas for garnishes are noted in many of the recipes.

These unique sandwich recipes take the simple Italian idea of grilling bread and turn it into a colorful world of flavors and textures. The variety of recipes in this book will allow you to enjoy panini all year long. With the right combination of fresh ingredients, delicious sides, savory spreads, and complementary beverages, all you need for a simple meal or snack is to pick a favorite recipe, assemble, grill, and enjoy!

farmers' market panini

three-cheese & tomato melt

This is the ultimate grilled cheese sandwich, filled with three melted cheeses, tangy tomato slices, and fresh basil. The freshness of ingredients is paramount in this simple sandwich, so seek out high-quality cheeses and the freshest produce you can find.

crusty country-style bread, 4 slices, each about 1/2 inch thick

extra-virgin olive oil, 1 tablespoon

garlic-and-herb cheese spread such as Boursin, or herbed fresh goat cheese, 3 tablespoons

mozzarella cheese, 2 ounces, thinly sliced

provolone cheese, 2 ounces, thinly sliced

ripe but firm tomato, 4 thin slices

large fresh basil leaves, 6

1 Preheat the sandwich grill. Place the bread slices on a work surface and brush 1 side of each with the olive oil. Turn and spread the unoiled sides with the herbed cheese, dividing it evenly. On each of 2 of the slices, layer one-fourth of the mozzarella, then one-fourth of the provolone, 2 tomato slices, and 3 basil leaves. Divide the remaining mozzarella and provolone on top. Place the remaining 2 bread slices on top, herbed-cheese sides down, and press to pack gently.

2 Place the panini in the grill, close the top plate, and cook until the bread is golden and toasted and the cheese is melted, 3–5 minutes. Cut each sandwich in half on the diagonal and serve right away.

serves two

make your own... Spreadable cheese can be found in well-stocked grocery stores. If you like, make your own by mixing cream cheese with chopped garlic and chopped fresh parsley, oregano, or other fresh herbs to taste.

grilled eggplant provençal

The texture of eggplant is softened when grilled. For a smoky flavor, grill the vegetable on an outdoor charcoal grill. Tapenade, a highly seasoned olive spread, is available jarred in Italian markets and most grocery stores. Use one made from black or green olives.

extra-virgin olive oil, 2 tablespoons

garlic, 1 clove, finely chopped

globe eggplant, 1 small, 4–6 ounces, trimmed and cut lengthwise into slices 1/2 inch thick

salt and freshly ground pepper

semolina rolls, 2, split, or 4 slices semolina bread, each about 1/2 inch thick

tapenade, 4 tablespoons

mozzarella cheese, 3 ounces, thinly sliced

ripe but firm tomato, 4 thin slices

1 Preheat the sandwich grill. In a small bowl, stir together the olive oil and garlic. Brush both sides of the eggplant slices with 1 tablespoon of the garlic oil. Put the eggplant in the grill, close the top plate, and cook until the eggplant is tender and grill marked, 3–5 minutes. Season to taste with salt and pepper. Transfer to a plate and set aside. (The eggplant can be grilled up to 3 hours ahead and kept at room temperature, or covered and refrigerated for up to 24 hours; if refrigerating, return to room temperature before assembling the panini.) Keep the sandwich grill on and wipe clean the grill plates.

2 Place the rolls, cut sides down, on a work surface and brush the crust sides of the rolls with the remaining 1 tablespoon garlic oil. Turn and spread the cut sides of the rolls with the tapenade, dividing it evenly, then layer one-fourth of the cheese, half of the eggplant, and 2 tomato slices over the tapenade on the bottom half of each roll. Divide the remaining cheese on top. Cover with the top halves of the rolls or the remaining 2 bread slices, tapenade sides down, and press to pack gently.

3 Place the panini in the grill, close the top plate, and cook until the bread is golden and toasted, the eggplant is hot, and the cheese is melted, 3–5 minutes. Cut each sandwich in half on the diagonal and serve right away.

serves two

greek salad

These panini feature all the traditional ingredients for a Greek salad folded into toasted pita breads. If the pita breads crowd the grill, cook one sandwich at a time. A romaine-heart salad dressed with vinaigrette is a nice accompaniment.

1 In a bowl, stir together the tomatoes, cucumber, olives, onion, mint, garlic, feta, pepper, and 1 tablespoon of the olive oil. Let stand at room temperature for 15 minutes to allow the flavors to blend.

2 Preheat the sandwich grill. Place the pita breads on a work surface and brush on both sides with the remaining 1 tablespoon olive oil. Spoon the vegetable mixture into the pockets of the breads, dividing it evenly and taking care not to open the seams of the pockets any more than necessary. Pat the breads lightly to distribute the mixture evenly.

3 Place the panini in the grill, close the top plate, and cook until the pita bread is crisped and golden and the vegetables and cheese are warmed through, 3–5 minutes. Cut each sandwich in half and serve right away. Pass the yogurt-mint mixture for dipping, if desired.

serves two

plum tomatoes, 1/4 cup diced

cucumber, 1/4 cup seeded and diced

Kalamata olives or other Greek olives, 3 tablespoons pitted and chopped

yellow onion, 2 tablespoons finely chopped

fresh mint, 2 tablespoons chopped

garlic, 1 clove, finely chopped

feta cheese, 3 ounces, crumbled

freshly ground pepper, 1/4 teaspoon

extra-virgin olive oil, 2 tablespoons

large pita breads, 2

plain yogurt, 1/4 cup, mixed with 1 tablespoon chopped fresh mint (optional)

asparagus, sun-dried tomato & goat cheese

The assertive tang of asparagus is nicely offset by the concentrated flavor of sun-dried tomatoes. Layers of soft goat cheese provide a flavorful "glue" for the sandwich. The addition of fresh spring herbs rounds out the flavors perfectly.

small French baguette, one, 6–8 ounces, split, or 2 white or whole-wheat French rolls, split

olive oil–packed sun-dried tomatoes, 1/4 cup drained and sliced, with 1 tablespoon oil reserved

soft goat cheese, 3 ounces, at room temperature

balsamic vinegar, 2 teaspoons

fresh chives, 2 tablespoons snipped

fresh thyme, 1 tablespoon chopped

blanched asparagus spears, 1/4 pound

1 Preheat the sandwich grill. Place the bread pieces, cut sides down, on a work surface and brush the crust sides with the reserved oil. Turn and spread the goat cheese on the cut sides of the bread, then sprinkle with the vinegar, chives, and thyme, dividing the ingredients evenly. Arrange half of the asparagus and half of the sun-dried tomatoes on each bottom half. Cover with the top halves, cheese sides down, and press to pack gently.

2 Place the panini in the grill, close the top plate, and cook until the bread is golden and toasted, the cheese is melted, and the asparagus is warm, 3–5 minutes. Cut each sandwich in half on the diagonal and serve right away.

serves two

blanching asparagus... To blanch asparagus, boil the spears in water to cover for 3–5 minutes, then transfer them to ice water to stop the cooking. Drain the asparagus, pat dry with paper towels, and use as directed.

tuscan white bean purée with bitter greens

Rough-textured country-style bread is the best counterpoint to the soft filling, which is flavored with garlic and lots of fresh herbs. If you like, you can also mash any leftover bean mixture and serve it open-faced as bruschetta, topped with diced tomatoes.

1 Bring a large pot three-fourths full of lightly salted water to a boil. Add the greens and cook until tender, 5–8 minutes. Drain in a colander, pressing with the back of a spoon to remove any excess liquid. Set aside.

2 In a frying pan, heat 2 tablespoons of the olive oil over medium heat. Add the garlic to the pan and cook, stirring, for about 15 seconds, then stir in the rosemary, thyme, oregano, and cayenne. Stir in the beans and 2 tablespoons broth. Reduce the heat to medium-low and cook, stirring with a wooden spoon and mashing the beans, until the beans are warmed through and the mixture forms a coarse purée, 3–5 minutes. If the mixture seems dry, add a bit more broth. Season with salt and black pepper to taste. Stir in the cooked greens. Let cool slightly.

3 Preheat the sandwich grill. Place the bread slices on a work surface and brush 1 side of each bread slice with the remaining 1 tablespoon olive oil. Turn the bread and divide the bean mixture evenly between 2 of the bread slices, spreading it about 1/2 inch thick. Layer the onion slices and cheese shavings over the bean mixture, dividing evenly. Cover with the remaining 2 bread slices, oiled sides up, and press to pack gently.

4 Place the panini in the grill, close the top plate, and cook until the bread is toasted and the beans and greens are warmed through, 3–5 minutes. Cut each sandwich in half and serve right away.

serves two

fresh turnip greens, 1/2 pound, washed and torn into small pieces

extra-virgin olive oil, 3 tablespoons

garlic, 2 cloves, minced

fresh rosemary, 2 teaspoons chopped

fresh thyme, 2 teaspoons chopped

fresh oregano, 2 teaspoons chopped

cayenne pepper, 1/4 teaspoon

white beans, 1 can (15 ounces), rinsed and drained

low-sodium chicken broth, 2–4 tablespoons

salt and freshly ground black pepper

whole-wheat country-style bread, 4 slices, each about 1/2 inch thick

red onion, 4 thin slices

pecorino romano cheese, 2 ounces, shaved with a vegetable peeler

summer vegetables with fresh basil

Many vegetables become even sweeter when grilled, as their natural sugars caramelize. Cooking them in a sandwich grill is quick and easy, requiring only that you slice all of the vegetables into an even thickness so they can cook at the same rate.

extra-virgin olive oil, 2 1/2 tablespoons

garlic, 1 clove, finely chopped

small yellow bell pepper, 1, seeded and cut into 6 wedges

small zucchini, 1, about 4 ounces, cut on the diagonal into slices about 1/4 inch thick

small red onion, 1/2, cut into slices about 1/4 inch thick

salt and freshly ground pepper

small French baguette, one, 6–8 ounces, split

Parmesan cheese, 2 ounces, shaved with a vegetable peeler

large fresh basil leaves, 8

1 Preheat the sandwich grill. In a small bowl, stir together the olive oil and garlic. Brush the bell pepper, zucchini, and onion with 1 1/2 tablespoons of the garlic oil. Season with salt and pepper. Put the vegetables in the grill, close the top plate, and cook until tender and lightly charred, 3–5 minutes. Transfer to a plate. (The vegetables can be grilled up to 3 hours ahead and kept at room temperature, or covered and refrigerated for up to 24 hours; if refrigerating, return to room temperature before assembling the panini.) Keep the sandwich grill on. There is no need to clean it, as the char from the vegetables adds flavor.

2 Place the baguette pieces, cut sides down, on a work surface and brush the crust sides with the remaining 1 tablespoon garlic oil. Turn the cut sides up and layer one-fourth of the cheese and 2 basil leaves on each bottom half, then divide the vegetables evenly between them. Top each with half of the remaining cheese and 2 basil leaves. Cover with the top halves, cut sides down, and press to pack gently.

3 Place the panini in the grill, close the top plate, and cook until the vegetables are hot, the cheese is softened and nearly melted, and the bread is golden with browned edges, 3–5 minutes. Cut each sandwich in half on the diagonal and serve right away.

serves two

cheddar cheese with apple & sage

The apple stays crisp and juicy in this delightful, autumnal recipe. Prepare it for breakfast with scrambled eggs, for lunch with tomato soup, or for dinner with a dressed vinaigrette salad. Apple butter can be found in the jam section of the grocery store.

1 Preheat the sandwich grill. Place the bread slices, cut sides down, on a work surface and brush 1 side of each bread slice with the oil. Turn and spread the unoiled side of 2 of the bread slices with the apple butter, dividing it evenly. Layer one-fourth of the cheese, half of the apple slices, and the sage over the apple butter on each, then divide the remaining cheese on top. Place the remaining 2 bread slices on top, oiled sides up, and press to pack gently.

2 Place the panini in the grill, close the top plate, and cook until the bread is golden and toasted, the cheese is melted, and the apple is warmed through and just beginning to soften, 3–5 minutes. Cut each sandwich in half on the diagonal and serve right away.

serves two

artisan walnut bread, 4 slices, each about 1/2 inch thick, or sage focaccia, 4 pieces, each about 4 inches square, halved horizontally

walnut oil, 1 tablespoon

apple butter, 2 tablespoons

Cheddar cheese, 3 ounces, thinly sliced

Granny Smith apple, 1, unpeeled, cored, and cut into slices about 1/4 inch thick

fresh sage, 1 tablespoon chopped

mushroom, spinach & fontina

Mixed mushrooms, from wild chanterelles to cultivated button mushrooms, add flair to this recipe and Cognac and fresh herbs enhance the natural flavors. Choose a sturdy bread that will contain the juicy mushrooms without falling apart.

unsalted butter, $2^1/_2$ tablespoons

mixed wild and cultivated mushrooms, 4 ounces, brushed clean and sliced

shallots, 2 tablespoons finely chopped

Cognac, 2 tablespoons

fresh tarragon, 1 tablespoon chopped

salt and freshly ground pepper

crusty country-style bread, 4 slices, each about $^1/_2$ inch thick

fontina cheese, 3 ounces, thinly sliced

baby spinach leaves, 1 cup

1 In a saucepan, melt $1^1/_2$ tablespoons of the butter over medium-high heat. Add the mushrooms and shallots and sauté until the mushrooms are softened and release their juices, 3–5 minutes. Continue to cook, stirring often, until most of the liquid is absorbed, 2–3 minutes longer. Stir in the Cognac, chopped tarragon, and salt and pepper to taste. Cook, stirring, for 1 minute. Let cool slightly. (Alternatively, allow the mixture to cool completely and refrigerate, covered, for up to 24 hours; reheat gently before assembling the panini.)

2 Preheat the sandwich grill. Melt the remaining 1 tablespoon butter in a small saucepan over medium-high heat. Place the bread slices on a work surface and brush 1 side of each with the melted butter. Turn and layer one-fourth of the cheese, half of the mushrooms, and half of the spinach on the unbuttered side of each of 2 of the bread slices. Divide the remaining cheese on top. Place the remaining 2 bread slices on top, buttered sides up, and press to pack gently.

3 Place the panini in the grill, close the top plate, and cook until the bread is golden and toasted, the spinach is wilted, and the cheese is melted, 3–5 minutes. Serve right away.

serves two

stuffed portobello mushrooms

Here, flat, palm-sized portobello mushrooms play the role of the bread, enclosing a filling of sweet bell peppers and herbed goat cheese. Serve this knife-and-fork preparation with store-bought ridged chips or Homemade Potato Chips (page 88).

extra-virgin olive oil, 2 tablespoons

garlic, 1 clove, finely chopped

red bell pepper, 1, seeded and cut into 8 wedges

green onions, 6, white and tender green parts only

salt and freshly ground pepper

portobello mushrooms, 4, each 3–4 inches in diameter, stems and gills removed

soft goat cheese, 3 ounces, at room temperature

fresh thyme, 2 teaspoons chopped

red wine vinegar, 2 teaspoons

1 Preheat the sandwich grill. In a small bowl, stir together the olive oil and garlic. Brush the bell pepper and green onions with 1/2 tablespoon of the garlic oil. Season with salt and pepper. Put the vegetables in the grill, close the top plate, and cook just until softened, 1–2 minutes for the onion and 3–5 minutes for the pepper. Transfer to a plate and set aside. (The vegetables can be grilled up to 3 hours ahead and kept at room temperature, or covered and refrigerated for up to 24 hours; if refrigerating, return to room temperature before assembling the panini.) Keep the sandwich grill on. There is no need to clean it, as the char from the vegetables adds flavor.

2 Using a sharp knife, cut a thin slice off the cap of each mushroom to make a flat top. Each mushroom should be no more than 3/4 inch thick. Brush the top and cavity of each mushroom cap with the remaining 1 1/2 tablespoons garlic oil and place on a work surface, hollow side up. Season with salt and pepper. Spread the cheese in the cavity of each mushroom, dividing it evenly, then sprinkle with the thyme. On 2 of the mushrooms, layer 4 of the bell pepper wedges and 3 of the green onions over the cheese. Drizzle with the vinegar. Top with the remaining mushrooms, cheese sides down, and press to pack gently.

3 Place the mushroom "sandwiches" in the grill. Close the top plate carefully so that the mushrooms don't slide. Cook until the mushrooms are tender and grill marked and the cheese is melted, 3–5 minutes. Serve right away.

serves two

pb & j

Grilling the bread and warming the peanut butter intensifies the flavor of both in this upscale peanut butter and jelly sandwich. Try artisan-crafted jams and preserves, such as morello cherry or mixed berry. A good-quality raspberry jelly will work just fine, too.

cinnamon bread or walnut bread, 4 slices, each about 1/2 inch thick

unsalted butter, 1 tablespoon, at room temperature

smooth or chunky natural peanut butter, 4 tablespoons

jam or preserves, 2 tablespoons

1 Preheat the sandwich grill. Place the bread slices on a work surface and spread 1 side of each with the butter. Turn and spread the unbuttered sides with the peanut butter, dividing it evenly, then spread the jam over the peanut butter on 2 of the slices. Place the remaining 2 bread slices on top, peanut butter sides down, and press to pack gently.

2 Place the panini in the grill, close the top plate, and cook until the bread is golden and toasted and the peanut butter is warmed and beginning to melt, 2–4 minutes. Cut each sandwich in half and serve right away.

serves two

serving ideas... Peanut butter and jelly sandwiches aren't just for lunch anymore. Serve this delicious treat for breakfast on the run or as a light supper accompanied by a salad of spinach, apples, dried cranberries, and walnuts.

poultry panini

rustic turkey with brie & apples

This easy panino integrates smoked turkey with rich Brie, crisp green apples, peppery watercress, and whole-wheat bread for an ideal texture, color, and taste combination. Fresh thyme and a drizzle of walnut oil lend it a sophisticated flair.

1 Preheat the sandwich grill. In a small bowl, stir together the oil and chopped thyme. Place the bread slices on a work surface and brush 1 side of each with the thyme oil. Turn 2 of the slices oiled side down and layer one-fourth of the Brie, half of the turkey, 3 slices of the apple, and a few sprigs of the watercress on the unoiled side of each. Drizzle with the lemon juice and the remaining 1 tablespoon thyme oil, dividing evenly, and sprinkle with pepper to taste. Divide the remaining Brie on top. Place the remaining 2 bread slices on top, oiled sides up, and press to pack gently.

2 Place the panini in the grill, close the top plate, and cook until the bread is golden and toasted, the apple and turkey are heated through, and the cheese is melted, 3–5 minutes. Cut each sandwich in half and serve right away with the remaining watercress and a few apple slices, if desired.

serves two

a seasonal switch... During the cold months of winter, when pears are at their peak, consider substituting a creamy, white Bosc pear or a juicy, sweet Comice pear for the apple. It will complement the Brie equally as well.

walnut oil, 2 tablespoons

fresh thyme, 2 teaspoons chopped

whole-wheat country-style bread, 4 slices, each about 1/2 inch thick

Brie cheese, 2 ounces, thinly sliced

smoked turkey, 2 ounces, thinly sliced

Granny Smith apple, unpeeled, 6 thin slices, plus more for garnish (optional)

watercress, 1 small bunch, tough stems removed

fresh lemon juice, 1/2 teaspoon

freshly ground pepper

turkey with cranberry compote

Here is a new take on Thanksgiving leftovers, but the easy compote can be made anytime fresh cranberries are available. A firm, dense pumpkin bread works well in the sandwich grill, taking on attractive ridge marks for this open-faced sandwich.

CRANBERRY COMPOTE

fresh cranberries, 1 1/2 cups (6 ounces)

Port wine, 1/3 cup

sugar, 1/3 cup

grated orange zest, 2 teaspoons

grated fresh ginger, 2 teaspoons

Dijon mustard, 1 tablespoon

mayonnaise, 3 tablespoons

fresh sage, 1 tablespoon chopped

firm pumpkin bread or pumpernickel bread, 2 slices, each about 1/2 inch thick

roasted turkey, 6 ounces, sliced

salt and freshly ground pepper

1 To make the compote, in a small saucepan, combine the cranberries, Port, and sugar. Bring to a boil over medium heat, stirring to dissolve the sugar. Stir in the orange zest and ginger. Reduce heat to medium-low and simmer until the berries have popped and the sauce is lightly thickened, 7–9 minutes. Let cool slightly before using. (The compote can be prepared up to 2 days ahead and refrigerated. Reheat gently before serving.)

2 Preheat the sandwich grill. In a small bowl, stir together the mustard, mayonnaise, and sage; set aside. Put the bread in the grill, close the top plate, and cook until lightly crisp and grill marked, 2–3 minutes.

3 Spread 1 side of each toasted bread slice with the mustard mixture. Place each on a plate. Top with the turkey slices, dividing them evenly. Season the turkey generously with salt and pepper. Spoon the warm cranberry compote over and around the bread. Serve right away.

serves two

turkey meatloaf with spicy tomato sauce

Meatloaf sandwiches are an old-fashioned lunch-box favorite. You can use any type of meatloaf, but turkey meatloaf is a lean choice. If you like, you can add arugula leaves to the sandwich before grilling it to contribute a peppery freshness.

SPICY TOMATO SAUCE

plum tomatoes, 4–6

yellow onion, 1

extra-virgin olive oil, 2 tablespoons

garlic, 2 cloves

dry white wine, 1/2 cup

capers, 1 1/2 tablespoons

red pepper flakes, 1/4 teaspoon

fresh oregano, 2 tablespoons chopped

salt and freshly ground black pepper

Aioli (page 89) or mayonnaise, 2 tablespoons

Dijon mustard, 2 tablespoons

fresh oregano, 1 tablespoon chopped

semolina bread, 4 slices, each about 1/2 inch thick

unsalted butter, 1 tablespoon

cooked turkey meatloaf, 2 thick slices

1 To make the tomato sauce, seed and chop the tomatoes (you should have about 2 1/2 cups) and chop the yellow onion. In a large frying pan, heat the olive oil over medium heat. Add the chopped onion and cook, stirring often, until just softened, about 4 minutes. Chop the garlic, add it to the pan, and cook, stirring, for 1 minute. Add the chopped tomatoes to the pan along with the wine, capers, and red pepper flakes. Bring to a boil, stirring often. Reduce the heat to medium-low, stir in the oregano, and simmer, uncovered, until the liquid is reduced to a chunky sauce, 4–6 minutes. Season to taste with salt and black pepper. Keep warm until ready to use. (Alternatively, let cool, cover, and refrigerate for up to 8 hours. Reheat gently before serving.)

2 Preheat a sandwich grill. In a small bowl, stir together the aioli, mustard, and 1 tablespoon oregano. Place the bread slices on a work surface and spread 1 side of each with the butter, then turn and spread the unbuttered sides with the aioli mixture. On 2 of the slices, place a meatloaf slice on top of the aioli. Place the remaining 2 bread slices on top, aioli sides down, and press to pack gently.

3 Place the panini in the grill, close the top plate, and cook until the bread is golden and toasted and the meatloaf is warmed through, 3–5 minutes. Cut each sandwich in half and place on individual plates. Ladle some tomato sauce over the panini and serve right away.

serves two

grilled chicken with tomato & mozzarella

This panino is deceptively easy. The lemony marinated chicken can be cooked on the sandwich grill. Success hinges on using the freshest basil and the ripest tomatoes, so make this recipe in the summer months, when the ingredients are at the height of freshness.

1 In a dish large enough to hold the chicken, combine 3 tablespoons of the olive oil, the lemon juice and zest, the garlic, salt, and red pepper flakes and whisk to mix well. Remove 1 tablespoon of the mixture. Place the cutlets in the dish with the marinade and turn to coat. Let stand at room temperature for 15 minutes. (Alternatively, cover and refrigerate for up to 1 hour, returning to room temperature before grilling.)

2 Preheat the sandwich grill. Remove the chicken from the marinade and discard the marinade. Arrange the cutlets in the grill, close the top plate, and cook until golden grill marks appear and the chicken is opaque throughout, about 5 minutes. (The chicken can be grilled in advance, covered, and refrigerated for up to 24 hours; return to room temperature before assembling the panini.) Keep the sandwich grill on and wipe clean the grill plates. Meanwhile, place the focaccia pieces, cut sides down, on a work surface and brush the crust sides with the remaining 1 tablespoon olive oil. Brush the cut sides with the reserved 1 tablespoon marinade. On 2 of the focaccia pieces, layer one-fourth of the cheese, followed by 1 cooked chicken cutlet, 2 tomato slices, and 3 basil leaves. Divide the remaining cheese on top. Place the remaining 2 focaccia pieces on top, marinade sides down, and press to pack gently.

3 Place the panini in the grill, close the top plate, and cook until the bread is golden and toasted and the cheese is melted, 3–5 minutes. Cut each sandwich in half and serve right away.

serves two

extra-virgin olive oil, 4 tablespoons

fresh lemon juice, 1 tablespoon

grated lemon zest, 1 teaspoon

garlic, 1 clove, finely chopped

salt, 1/4 teaspoon

red pepper flakes, 1/8 teaspoon

boneless chicken breast cutlets, 2, about 4 ounces each, flattened to about 1/2 inch thick

focaccia, 2 pieces, each about 4 inches square, halved horizontally

mozzarella cheese, 2 ounces, thinly sliced

ripe but firm tomato, 4 thin slices

large fresh basil leaves, 6

curried chicken salad on grilled cornbread

Chicken salad and cornbread are both southern favorites. Use cornbread that is dense and firm, not soft and cakey, and not too sweet; if making your own, choose a recipe that's low in sugar. This open-faced sandwich is perfect for lunch or a light summer supper.

1 Place the walnuts in a small, dry skillet over medium-low heat. Cook, stirring constantly, until lightly toasted and fragrant, 5–7 minutes; watch carefully, as they can burn quickly. Transfer immediately to a cutting board to cool, then chop coarsely.

2 In a bowl, stir together the mayonnaise, mustard, lemon juice, and curry powder. Stir in the chicken, toasted walnuts, onion, raisins, celery, apple, and chopped mint. Season to taste with salt and pepper. Let the chicken salad stand at room temperature for 15 minutes to allow the flavors to blend. (Alternatively, cover and refrigerate for up to 6 hours; return to room temperature before assembling the panini.)

3 Preheat a sandwich grill. Put the cornbread in the grill, close the top plate, and cook until golden and toasted, 2–3 minutes. Place 2 pieces of the toasted bread on each of 2 individual plates. Heap the chicken salad on the bread, dividing it evenly, and serve right away.

serves two

walnut halves, 1/4 cup

mayonnaise, 1/3 cup

Dijon mustard, 1 tablespoon

fresh lemon juice, 1 teaspoon

curry powder, 1/4 teaspoon

cooked chicken breast, 1 cup diced

red onion, 3 tablespoons chopped

raisins, 2 tablespoons

celery, 2 tablespoons coarsely chopped

Granny Smith apple, unpeeled, 1/4 cup diced

fresh mint, 1 tablespoon chopped

salt and freshly ground pepper

firm cornbread, 4 slices, each about 1/2 inch thick

southwestern chicken quesadilla

Flour tortillas fold easily to enclose flavorful fillings and are made with oil, which helps them brown nicely. Quesadillas are a great way to use leftover grilled or roasted chicken, or a shredded purchased rotisserie chicken, making quick work of a lunch or dinner.

cooked chicken, 3/4 cup shredded

cooked corn kernels, 1/3 cup

roasted poblano pepper, 3 tablespoons chopped

green onion, 3 tablespoons chopped

fresh cilantro, 2 tablespoons chopped

sour cream, 2 tablespoons

chipotle chile powder, 3/4 teaspoon

salt, 1/4 teaspoon

flour tortillas, two, 8 or 10 inches in diameter

corn oil or melted unsalted butter, 2 teaspoons

jack cheese, with or without jalapeños, 3 ounces, shredded

Fresh Tomato Salsa for serving (page 89)

lime wedges for serving

1 Preheat the sandwich grill. In a bowl, stir together the chicken, corn, peppers, green onion, cilantro, sour cream, 1/2 teaspoon of the chile powder, and the salt. Place the tortillas on a work surface, brush 1 side of each with the oil, and sprinkle with the remaining 1/4 teaspoon chile powder. Turn the tortillas over and spoon the chicken mixture onto half of each tortilla, dividing it evenly and leaving a 1/2-inch border around the edges. Sprinkle each with half of the cheese. Fold the tortillas over the filling and lightly press the edges together to help them adhere.

2 Place the quesadillas in the grill, close the top plate, and cook until the filling is hot and the cheese is melted. Cut each quesadilla into wedges, transfer to individual plates, and serve right away, passing the tomato salsa and lime wedges at the table.

serves two

mix it up... You can substitute nearly any combination of ingredients for the ones used here. Try using cooked, shredded pork instead of chicken, roasted bell peppers or zucchini for the corn, or Cheddar cheese for the jack.

chicken & mango with cilantro pesto

This pesto, redolent of Carribean-style flavors, is a flavorful twist on a sandwich spread. Use any extra pesto to toss with pasta or stir into chicken soup for a burst of flavor. Substitute shredded cooked pork or beef or cooked shrimp for the chicken, if you like.

1 To make the pesto, place the pine nuts in a small, dry skillet over medium-low heat. Cook, stirring constantly, until lightly toasted, 3–5 minutes; watch carefully, as they can burn quickly. Transfer immediately to a plate to cool. Seed and chop the jalapeño. In a food processor, combine the toasted pine nuts, chopped jalapeño, cilantro, green onion, garlic, and salt. Process to a coarse purée. With the motor running, slowly pour in the olive oil and process to a smooth purée. Add the cheese and lime juice and pulse to blend. (You can keep the pesto tightly covered in the refrigerator for up to 2 days or in the freezer for up to 1 month.)

2 Preheat the sandwich grill. In a bowl, stir together the chicken, mayonnaise, and jerk sauce. In a small bowl, stir together the oil and allspice. Place the rolls, cut sides down, on a work surface and brush the crust sides with the seasoned oil. Turn and spread the cut sides with about 1/4 cup of the pesto, reserving the remaining pesto for another use. Spoon the chicken mixture onto the bottom halves of the rolls, dividing it evenly. Top each with 3 slices of mango and 2 slices of onion. Cover with the top halves of the rolls, pesto sides down, and press to pack gently.

3 Place the panini in the grill, close the top plate, and cook until the bread is golden and toasted and the chicken and mango are warmed through, 3–5 minutes. Cut each sandwich in half, if desired, and serve right away.

serves two

CILANTRO PESTO

pine nuts, 1/4 cup

small jalapeño, 1

fresh cilantro leaves, 1 1/2 cups

green onion, 1/4 cup chopped

garlic, 2 cloves

salt, 1/2 teaspoon

extra-virgin olive oil, 1/2 cup

jack cheese, 1/4 cup grated

fresh lime juice, 2 teaspoons

cooked chicken, 1 cup shredded

mayonnaise, 2 tablespoons

Caribbean jerk sauce, 2 teaspoons

extra-virgin olive oil, 1 tablespoon

allspice, 1/4 teaspoon

Cuban rolls, 2, split

fresh mango, 6 slices

red onion, 4 thin slices

seafood panini

grilled salmon with chipotle aioli

Cornmeal-accented yeast bread is best for this Southwestern-style sandwich, but Cuban rolls or crusty French bread are also delicious with the spicy aioli. Chipotles in adobo are deceptively hot, so use the minimum at first, then taste and add more if you wish.

1 To make the aioli, finely chop the garlic. In a small bowl, stir together the mayonnaise and olive oil until smooth, then stir in 1 teaspoon of the chipotles in adobo, the garlic, and the lime juice until blended. Let stand for 15 minutes at room temperature to allow the flavors to blend. Taste the aioli and add more chipotles in adobo, if needed.

2 Preheat the sandwich grill. Use your hand to gently flatten the salmon fillets to an even thickness of about 1/2 inch. Brush the salmon on both sides with 1/2 tablespoon of the olive oil and the lime juice, then sprinkle with 1 teaspoon of the lime zest and salt and pepper to taste. Arrange the fillets in the grill, close the top plate, and cook until the salmon is just opaque throughout and grill marked, 3–5 minutes. Transfer the salmon to a plate and set aside. Keep the sandwich grill on and wipe clean the grill plates.

3 Place the bread slices, cut sides down, on a work surface and brush 1 side of each bread slice with the remaining 1 tablespoon olive oil, then sprinkle with the remaining 1 teaspoon lime zest, patting lightly to help it adhere. In a bowl, toss the greens with the cilantro. Turn the bread and spread the aioli on the unoiled sides, then place 1 salmon fillet on each of 2 slices. Divide the greens evenly on top. Cover with the remaining 2 slices, aioli sides down, and press to pack gently. Cook until the bread is toasted and crusty and the greens are barely wilted, 2–4 minutes. Serve right away.

serves two

CHIPOTLE AIOLI

garlic, 1 clove

mayonnaise, 3 tablespoons

extra-virgin olive oil, 1/2 tablespoon

chipotle chiles in adobo, 1–2 teaspoons mashed

fresh lime juice, 1 teaspoon

salmon fillets, 2, about 5 ounces each

extra-virgin olive oil, 1 1/2 tablespoons

fresh lime juice, 1 teaspoon

lime zest, 2 teaspoons grated

salt and freshly ground pepper

crusty country-style bread, 4 slices, each about 1/2 inch thick

mixed baby salad greens, 1 cup

fresh cilantro, 2 tablespoons chopped

asian ahi tuna

Also known as yellowfin, fresh sushi-grade tuna is commonly also called ahi. It is important to use high-quality tuna for these sandwiches, since the fish is not cooked through. Find sliced pickled ginger and five-spice powder in the Asian-food section of the grocery store.

mayonnaise, 1/4 cup

wasabi powder, 2 teaspoons

green onion, 2 tablespoons chopped

ahi tuna steaks, 2, each 5–6 ounces and about 3/4 inch thick

sesame oil, 2 tablespoons

five-spice powder, 1/2 teaspoon

sesame seed rolls, 2, split

pickled ginger, 2 tablespoons

watercress, 1 small bunch, tough stems removed

1 In a small bowl, stir together the mayonnaise and wasabi powder until well blended, then stir in the green onion. Set aside. Rub the tuna steaks with 1 tablespoon of the sesame oil, then sprinkle with 1/4 teaspoon of the five-spice powder. Let the wasabi mayonnaise and the tuna steaks stand for 15 minutes at room temperature to allow the flavors to blend, or cover and refrigerate for up to 1 hour; if refrigerating, return to room temperature before grilling the tuna and assembling the panini.

2 Preheat the sandwich grill. Arrange the tuna steaks in the grill, close the top plate, and cook until seared on the outside and about 1/4 inch into the interior, 8–10 minutes. Transfer immediately to a plate. Leave the grill on and clean the grill plates.

3 Place the rolls, cut sides down, on a work surface and brush the crust sides with the remaining 1 tablespoon sesame oil, then sprinkle with the remaining 1/4 teaspoon five-spice powder. Turn and spread the wasabi mayonnaise on the cut side of each roll, then layer 1 tuna steak, half of the pickled ginger, and half of the watercress over the mayonnaise on the bottom half of each roll. Cover with the top halves of the rolls, mayonnaise sides down, and press to pack gently. Place the panini in the grill, close the top plate, and cook until the bread is golden and toasted, the ginger and tuna are warmed through, and the watercress is just slightly wilted, 2–4 minutes. The tuna should not cook much further. Place on warmed plates and serve at once.

serves two

tuna niçoise

Sunny Mediterranean flavors infuse this sandwich inspired by the classic Niçoise salad. If time permits, the panini is even better when it is assembled about 1 hour before it is grilled. This will allow the juices of the filling to seep into the bread, adding flavor.

1 In a bowl, combine the tuna, fennel, olives, capers, and anchovy and toss with a fork to mix well, breaking up the tuna. Add the lemon juice, mayonnaise, and basil and stir to blend. Season to taste with salt and pepper.

2 Place the rolls, cut sides up, on a work surface. Divide the tuna mixture between the bottom halves of the rolls, then layer 2 tomato slices, 2 onion slices, and half of the arugula on top of each. Cover with the top halves of the rolls and press to pack gently. Wrap the panini in aluminum foil and let stand at room temperature for 15 minutes to allow the flavors to blend, or cover and refrigerate for up to 1 hour; if refrigerating, return to room temperature before grilling.

3 Preheat the sandwich grill. Unwrap the panini and brush the crust sides with the reserved oil. Place the panini in the grill, close the top plate, and cook until the bread is golden and toasted and the tuna salad is warmed through, 3–5 minutes. Serve right away.

serves two

olive oil–packed tuna, 1 can (6 ounces), drained, with 1 tablespoon oil reserved

fennel bulb, 1/4 cup coarsely chopped

Niçoise olives or other small black, brine-cured olives, 2 tablespoons chopped

capers, 2 teaspoons

anchovy, 1, mashed

fresh lemon juice, 2 teaspoons

mayonnaise, 3 tablespoons

fresh basil, 1 tablespoon chopped

salt and freshly ground pepper

French rolls, 2, split

ripe but firm tomato, 4 thin slices

red onion, 4 thin slices

arugula leaves, 1/2 cup stemmed

spicy tuna bocadillo

This flavorful sandwich takes its inspiration from the tapas bars of Spain. The spiced tuna and the sprightly lemon aioli burst with flavor, while the egg and arugula provide colorful and toothsome layers. For extra flavor, you can cook the tuna on an outdoor grill.

1 Finely chop the garlic. In a shallow dish, combine 1 tablespoon of the olive oil, half of the chopped garlic, 1 tablespoon of the lemon juice, 1/2 teaspoon of the zest, the oregano, thyme, paprika, cumin, cardamom, cayenne, and salt and pepper to taste. Whisk to mix well. Add the tuna, turn to coat, and let stand for about 15 minutes at room temperature to allow the flavors to blend. (Or, cover and refrigerate for up to 1 hour; return to room temperature before grilling.)

2 In a small bowl, stir together the mayonnaise, 1 tablespoon of the olive oil, the remaining garlic, and the remaining 1 tablespoon lemon juice and 1/2 teaspoon lemon zest. Cover and refrigerate for up to 4 hours. Return to room temperature before assembling the panini.

3 Preheat the sandwich grill. Arrange the tuna steaks in the grill, close the top plate, and cook, turning once, until seared on the outside and pink on the inside, 3–5 minutes. Transfer to a cutting board, let cool slightly, then slice thinly. Leave the grill on and wipe clean the grill plates.

4 Brush the crust sides of the rolls with the remaining 1 tablespoon olive oil and spread the cut sides with aioli. On the bottom half of each, arrange a layer each of the tuna, pepper, onion, eggs, and arugula, dividing evenly. Cover with the top halves of the rolls, cut sides down, and press to pack gently. Place the panini in the grill, close the top plate, and cook until the bread is golden and toasted and the filling is warmed, 3–5 minutes. Cut in half and serve right away.

serves two

garlic, 2 cloves

extra-virgin olive oil, 3 tablespoons

fresh lemon juice, 2 tablespoons

lemon zest, 1 teaspoon grated

fresh oregano and fresh thyme, 2 teaspoons chopped *each*

paprika, 1 teaspoon

ground cumin, ground cardamom, and cayenne pepper 1/4 teaspoon *each*

salt and freshly ground black pepper

tuna steaks, 2, each about 6 ounces

mayonnaise, 3 tablespoons

Portuguese rolls, 2, split

roasted red pepper, 1/4 cup sliced

sweet onion, 4 slices

hard-boiled eggs, 2, sliced

arugula leaves, 1/2 cup

crab melt

This hybrid sandwich marries two East-Coast classics. The roll is New England's specialty bun used for Maine's lobster rolls. The filling is pure Chesapeake Bay, laced with well-seasoned crabmeat; find Old Bay brand seasoning in the spice section of most markets.

mayonnaise, 1/4 cup

fennel bulb, 3 tablespoons finely chopped

green onion, 3 tablespoons thinly sliced

fresh lemon juice, 2 teaspoons

lemon zest, 1/2 teaspoon grated

Old Bay seasoning or other Chesapeake Bay–seafood seasoning, 1 teaspoon

fresh lump crabmeat, 8 ounces, picked over for shell fragments

hot dog buns, 2, preferably New England–cut

unsalted butter, 1 tablespoon, melted

Cheddar cheese, 2 ounces, shredded (optional)

Homemade Potato Chips for serving (page 88; optional)

1 In a small bowl, stir together the mayonnaise, fennel, green onion, lemon juice and zest, and Old Bay seasoning until well blended. Gently stir in the crabmeat, taking care not to break it up too much.

2 Preheat the sandwich grill. Open the hot dog buns flat and brush on all sides with the melted butter. Place in the grill, close the top plate, and cook until lightly toasted, 2–3 minutes. If using the cheese, leave the buns in the grill and heap the crab salad into them, dividing it evenly, then sprinkle with cheese. Lower the top to within 1/2 inch of the cheese and hold until melted, 30–40 seconds. If not using the cheese, simply transfer the toasted buns to warmed plates, heap the crab salad into them, and serve at once with a handful of potato chips, if desired.

serves two

the traditional roll... New England hot dog buns are distinguished by their split tops and the lack of crust on their sides. Find them in specialty-food stores. You can also substitute a standard hot dog bun for the traditional roll.

shrimp po'boy

Po'boys are the traditional submarine sandwiches from New Orleans. This version features classic sweet, fried shrimp and tart mayonnaise dressing, but the submarine roll is grilled in the sandwich maker for added texture. If you like, garnish it with hot-pepper sauce.

RÉMOULADE SAUCE

capers, 1 teaspoon

mayonnaise, 1/2 cup

tomato paste, 2 teaspoons

Dijon mustard, 2 teaspoons

vinegar, 1 teaspoon

fresh chives, 1 tablespoon snipped

cornichons, 1 tablespoon chopped

fresh flat-leaf parsley, 1 tablespoon chopped

fresh tarragon, 2 teaspoons chopped

yellow cornmeal, 1/4 cup

salt, 1/4 teaspoon

cayenne pepper, 1/8 teaspoon

large shrimp, 1/2 pound

canola oil for frying, plus 1 tablespoon

submarine rolls, 2, split

iceberg lettuce, 1/2 cup shredded

1 To make the rémoulade sauce, chop the capers coarsely. In a small bowl, stir together the mayonnaise, tomato paste, mustard, and vinegar until smooth. Stir in the chives, cornichons, parsley, tarragon, and chopped capers. Let stand at room temperature for about 15 minutes to allow the flavors to blend. (Alternatively, cover and refrigerate for up to 24 hours; if refrigerating, return to room temperature before serving.)

2 Preheat the oven to 200°F. Stir together the cornmeal, salt, and cayenne on a small, rimmed plate. Peel and devein the shrimp, then place them on the plate, half at a time, and turn to coat completely with the cornmeal. In a deep frying pan or saucepan, heat 2 inches of oil to 375°F on a deep-frying thermometer. Working in 2 batches to avoid crowding, add the shrimp and fry until golden, crisp, and opaque throughout, about 1 1/2 minutes per batch. Let the oil return to 375°F between batches. Using a slotted spoon, transfer the shrimp to paper towels to drain. If not using immediately, keep warm in a single layer in the oven.

3 Preheat the sandwich grill. Cut the rolls in half horizontally and place on a work surface. Brush on both sides with the 1 tablespoon canola oil. Put the rolls in the grill, close the top plate, and cook until golden and toasted, 2–3 minutes. Spread the cut sides of 2 of the roll halves with a thin coating of the rémoulade sauce and top with the shrimp and shredded lettuce, dividing evenly. Top each with the other 2 roll halves, pressing gently to pack the ingredients. Serve right away.

serves two

meaty panini

all-american roast beef

If you can find a purveyor of extra-tender, rare roast beef, or you have some leftover, this is a perfect use for it. The sandwich grill heats the meat but doesn't overcook it, and barely wilts the watercress. Round out the meal with Shoestring Fries (page 88) and a green salad.

1 In a small bowl, stir together the mayonnaise, sour cream, horseradish, and marjoram. Let stand for about 10 minutes at room temperature to allow the flavors to blend. (Alternatively, cover and refrigerate for up to 6 hours; if refrigerating, return to room temperature before using.)

2 Preheat the sandwich grill. Place the bread slices, cut sides down, on a work surface and spread 1 side of each bread slice with the butter. Turn and spread the unbuttered sides of the bread with the mayonnaise mixture. On each of 2 of the bread slices, mayonnaise sides up, arrange half of the roast beef. Season liberally with salt and pepper. Divide the cheese and the watercress on top. Cover with the remaining 2 bread slices or the top halves of the rolls, mayonnaise sides down, and press to pack gently.

3 Place the panini in the grill, close the top plate, and cook until the bread is golden and toasted, the meat is warmed through, and the watercress is nearly wilted, 3–5 minutes. Cut each sandwich in half on the diagonal and serve right away.

serves two

mayonnaise, 3 tablespoons

sour cream, 1 tablespoon

prepared horseradish, 1 tablespoon

fresh marjoram, 1 tablespoon chopped

whole-wheat country-style bread or rye bread, 4 slices, or 2 ciabatta sandwich rolls, split

unsalted butter, 1 tablespoon, at room temperature

roast beef, 1/2 pound, thinly sliced

salt and freshly ground pepper

Parmesan cheese, 1 ounce, shaved with a vegetable peeler

watercress, 1 small bunch, tough stems removed

italian-style cheesesteak

This Italian version of the famous Philly cheesesteak uses high-quality beef, rich fontina, and bright, fresh, herb pesto. If desired, you can use a high-quality purchased pesto. You can freeze the pesto, tightly covered, for up to 1 month.

BASIL PESTO

pine nuts, 1/4 cup

fresh basil leaves, 2 cups tightly packed

garlic, 2 cloves, chopped

extra-virgin olive oil, 3 tablespoons

Parmesan cheese, 1/4 cup grated

salt and freshly ground pepper

extra-virgin olive oil, 1/4 cup

yellow onion, 1, sliced

small red bell pepper, 1, seeded and sliced

garlic, 2 cloves, chopped

balsamic vinegar, 1 tablespoon

salt and freshly ground pepper

thin, tender skirt steak, 10 ounces

long Italian rolls, 2, split

fontina cheese, 4 ounces, thinly sliced

1 To make the pesto, place the pine nuts in a small, dry skillet over medium-low heat. Cook, stirring constantly, until lightly toasted, 3–5 minutes; watch carefully, as they can burn quickly. Transfer to a plate to cool. In a food processor, combine the nuts and basil. With the motor running, add the garlic to the machine. Pulse to finely chop. With the motor running, slowly pour in the olive oil and process to a purée. Add the cheese and pulse to blend. Season with salt and pepper. Set aside.

2 In a frying pan, heat 2 tablespoons of the olive oil over medium heat. Add the onion, bell pepper, and garlic and cook, stirring, until the vegetables are tender, 5–8 minutes. Remove from the heat, stir in the vinegar, and season to taste with salt and pepper. Set aside.

3 Preheat the sandwich grill. Season the steak with salt and pepper. Arrange the steak in the grill, close the top plate, and cook the steak until charred on the outside and medium-rare on the inside, 3–4 minutes. Transfer the steak to a plate and set aside. Keep the sandwich grill on and wipe clean the grill plates. Place the rolls, cut sides down, on a work surface and brush the crust with the remaining 1 tablespoon olive oil. Spread the cut sides with 1/4 cup of pesto. On the bottom halves, pesto sides up, layer the steak, cheese, and onions and peppers, dividing evenly. Cover with the top halves, pesto sides down, and press to pack gently.

4 Place the panini in the grill, close the top plate, and cook until the bread is toasted, the beef is warmed, and the cheese is melted, 3–5 minutes. Cut each sandwich in half and serve right away.

serves two

chorizo with manchego

Made with spicy Spanish chorizo and assertive Manchego cheese, this sandwich also features sweet roasted red peppers and peppery arugula. Sprinkling the bread with smoked paprika before grilling adds even more smoky flavor.

1 In a frying pan, heat the oil over medium-high heat. Add the chorizo and sauté until crisp on the edges, 3–4 minutes. Transfer to paper towels to drain, reserving the drippings in the pan.

2 Preheat the sandwich grill. Place the rolls, cut sides down, on a work surface. Brush the crust sides of the rolls with the reserved oil, then sprinkle with the paprika. Turn the bottom halves of the rolls, oiled sides down and layer one-fourth of the cheese and half each of the chorizo, cilantro, red pepper, and arugula on the unoiled sides. Top each with half of the remaining cheese. Cover with the top halves of the rolls, oiled sides up, and press to pack gently.

3 Place the panini in the grill, close the top plate, and cook until the bread is golden and toasted and the cheese is melted, 3–5 minutes. Cut each sandwich in half and serve right away.

serves two

extra-virgin olive oil, 1 tablespoon

Spanish chorizo links, 1/4 pound, thinly sliced crosswise

Portuguese rolls, 2, split, or 4 slices crusty Italian or Spanish bread, each about 1/2 inch thick

Spanish smoked paprika, 1/2 teaspoon

Manchego cheese, 3 ounces, thinly sliced

fresh cilantro, 2 tablespoons chopped

roasted red pepper, 1/4 cup sliced

arugula leaves, 1 cup, stemmed

muffuletta

The classic muffuletta sandwich is a large, round Sicilian loaf filled with a salad of olives, celery, carrots, and cauliflower, and heaped with meats and cheeses. This recipe makes smaller, individual versions. Look for the olive salad at an Italian deli.

round Italian rolls, 2, split, or 4 slices Sicilian-style sourdough bread, each about 1/2 inch thick

extra-virgin olive oil, 1 tablespoon

Sicilian-style mixed olive salad, 1/2 cup

mortadella, 2 ounces, thinly sliced

provolone cheese, 2 ounces, thinly sliced

capicola or other Italian ham, 2 ounces, thinly sliced

mozzarella cheese, 2 ounces, thinly sliced

1 Preheat the sandwich grill. Place the rolls, cut sides down, on a work surface and brush the crust sides with the olive oil. Turn, oiled sides down, and divide the olive salad between the bottom halves of the rolls. Layer half each of the mortadella, provolone, capicola, and mozzarella on top. Cover with the top halves of the rolls, oiled sides up, and press to pack gently.

2 Place the panini in the grill, close the top plate, and cook until the bread is golden and toasted, the meats are warmed, and the cheese is nearly melted, 3–5 minutes. Cut each sandwich into quarters and serve right away.

serves two

a Louisiana classic... Muffulettas were invented in 1906, at a Sicilian bakery in New Orleans. Despite the popularity of the other regional favorite, po'boys, these are the oldest and most traditional sandwiches from the area.

mediterranean spiced lamb

This panini is based on a gyro, a favorite street food throughout Greece and the Middle East. Usually made with seasoned, skewered, and grilled lamb, the meat is heaped into pita breads along with chopped onion and tomato, then folded to make it easy to eat.

1 In a small bowl, stir together the yogurt, lemon juice, garlic, rosemary, oregano, lemon zest, salt, and red pepper flakes. Pour half of the yogurt mixture into a shallow dish just large enough to hold the lamb; reserve the remaining mixture to use as a sauce. Add the lamb and stir to coat with the yogurt mixture. Cover and refrigerate for at least 2 hours or up to 6 hours. Return to room temperature before grilling.

2 Prepare a fire in a charcoal grill or preheat a gas grill to high. Thread the lamb cubes onto metal skewers. Grill over direct heat, turning once or twice, until lightly charred on the outside and cooked to medium or medium-rare on the inside, 4–6 minutes. Transfer to a platter, cover loosely with aluminum foil, and set aside.

3 Preheat the sandwich grill. Place the pita breads on a work surface and brush one side with the olive oil. Spoon the lamb evenly onto one side of each pita round. Top generously with the tomato, cucumber, and green onions, dividing them evenly. Fold the pita in half to contain the filling. Press the folded pita to pack gently.

4 Place the panini in the grill, close the top plate, and cook until the pitas are crisped and golden and the vegetables and cheese are warmed through, 2–4 minutes. Serve right away, garnished with any remaining tomatoes, cucumbers, or green onions. Pass the reserved yogurt mixture to use as a sauce.

serves two

plain yogurt, $^3/_4$ cup

fresh lemon juice, 2 tablespoons

garlic, 2 cloves, finely chopped

fresh rosemary, 1 tablespoon chopped

fresh oregano, 1 tablespoon chopped

lemon zest, 1 teaspoon grated

salt, $^1/_2$ teaspoon

red pepper flakes, $^1/_4$ teaspoon

boneless lamb from the leg or loin, 10 ounces, cut into $1^1/_2$-inch cubes

whole-wheat pita breads, 2

extra-virgin olive oil, 1 tablespoon

ripe but firm tomato, $^1/_2$ cup seeded and diced

cucumber, $^1/_2$ cup seeded and diced

green onion, $^1/_2$ cup thinly sliced

the reuben

The Reuben is a quintessential New York City sandwich. Whether you choose rye or pumpernickel bread, seeded or not, the sandwich must contain good corned beef, Swiss cheese, a spoonful of fresh sauerkraut, and the best Russian dressing that you can find.

rye bread or pumpernickel bread, 4 slices, each about 1/2 inch thick

unsalted butter, 1 tablespoon, melted

Russian dressing, preferably homemade (see below), 1/4 cup

Jarlsburg cheese, 3 ounces, thinly sliced

corned beef, 4 ounces, thinly sliced

fresh sauerkraut, 1/3 cup, drained

1 Preheat the sandwich grill. Place the bread slices on a work surface and brush 1 side of each with the melted butter, then turn and spread the unbuttered sides with the Russian dressing. On each of 2 of the bread slices, layer one-fourth of the cheese, half of the corned beef, and half of the sauerkraut. Top each with the remaining cheese, dividing it evenly. Place the remaining 2 bread slices on top, dressing sides down, and press to pack gently.

2 Place the panini in the grill, close the top plate, and cook until the bread is golden and toasted and the cheese is melted, 3–5 minutes. Cut each sandwich in half and serve right away.

serves two

homemade dressing... To make Russian dressing, combine 1/4 cup mayonnaise and 2 teaspoons ketchup with 1/2 teaspoon minced onion, 1/4 teaspoon Worcestershire sauce, 1/4 teaspoon horseradish, and 2 teaspoons minced parsley.

eggs & bacon breakfast sandwich

This traditional morning treat is made better with grilling and the addition of fresh herbs. English muffins or crusty whole-wheat slices are the breads of choice, but you can serve this sandwich any way you like. Pass hot-pepper sauce for sprinkling.

thick-cut bacon, 4 slices

unsalted butter, 2 tablespoons, at room temperature

large eggs, 4

salt and freshly ground pepper

fresh tarragon, 3 teaspoons chopped

English muffins, 2, split, or 4 slices whole-wheat country-style bread, each about 1/2 inch thick

Cheddar cheese, 2 ounces, thinly sliced

1 In a frying pan over medium heat, fry the bacon until crisp, 8–10 minutes. Transfer to paper towels to drain. Pour off and discard the bacon drippings.

2 In the same frying pan, melt 1 tablespoon of the butter. When the butter is hot and foamy, crack the eggs into the pan. Cook over medium heat until the whites look opaque and set with crisped brown edges, but the yolks are still somewhat runny, 3–4 minutes. Season with salt, pepper, and 2 teaspoons of the chopped tarragon. Using a metal spatula, flip the eggs, taking care not to break the yolks. Cook until the yolks are softly set, about 30 seconds longer.

3 Preheat the sandwich grill. Spread the remaining 1 tablespoon butter on both sides of the English muffins. Put the muffins, cut sides down, in the grill and cook until lightly toasted on one side, 1–2 minutes. Turn, toasted side up, in the grill. On each muffin bottom, layer one-fourth of the cheese and 1 egg. Top with the remaining cheese on each. Cover with the muffin tops, toasted sides down. Sprinkle the untoasted bread with the remaining 1 teaspoon chopped tarragon.

4 Close the top plate and cook until the bread is toasted and the cheese is melted, 4–5 minutes. Cut each sandwich in half and serve right away.

serves two

prosciutto with fig jam

This sandwich is outstanding with walnut-studded rustic bread, found in artisan bakeries. Other good bread options are cranberry yeast bread (not quick bread) or even olive bread. Fig jam is available in well-stocked supermarkets or Mediterranean-food stores.

1 In a frying pan, heat the olive oil over high heat. Add the prosciutto and cook, turning once or twice, until the edges begin to crisp and curl, 1–2 minutes. Transfer to paper towels to drain. Reserve the oil in the frying pan.

2 Preheat the sandwich grill. Place the bread slices on a work surface. Brush 1 side of the bread slices with the oil in the frying pan. Turn and spread the unoiled sides with the jam. On each of 2 of the bread slices, jam sides up, layer half of the prosciutto and Gorgonzola. Place the remaining 2 bread slices on top, jam sides down, and press to pack gently.

3 Place the panini in the grill, close the top plate, and cook until the bread is golden and toasted and the cheese is melted, 3–5 minutes. Cut each sandwich in half and serve right away.

serves two

extra-virgin olive oil, 1 tablespoon

prosciutto, 2 ounces, thinly sliced

walnut bread or other flavorful artisan yeast bread, 4 slices, each about 1/2 inch thick

fig jam, 4 tablespoons

Gorgonzola cheese, 3 tablespoons, crumbled

croque-monsieur

This panino, based on the classic French sandwich, features lean ham, sliced cheese, and a rich, flavorful cheese sauce. For the best results, put the sandwich under the broiler for a few seconds before serving to brown the top.

CHEESE SAUCE

unsalted butter, 2 tablespoons

all-purpose flour, 2 tablespoons

Dijon mustard, 2 teaspoons

grated nutmeg, 1/4 teaspoon

salt and freshly ground pepper

whole milk, 1 cup

Gruyère cheese, 1/4 cup shredded

French bread or other firm, white country-style bread, 4 slices, each about 1/2 inch thick

unsalted butter, 1 tablespoon, melted

Dijon mustard, 1 tablespoon

Gruyère cheese, 1/4 pound, thinly sliced

Black Forest ham, 3 ounces, thinly sliced

fresh chives, 2 teaspoons snipped

1 To make the cheese sauce, in a small saucepan, melt the butter over medium heat. Add the flour and cook, whisking, for 1 minute to make a smooth paste. Stir in the mustard, nutmeg, and salt and pepper to taste, then slowly whisk in the milk. Cook, whisking, until the sauce comes to a boil and thickens, about 2 minutes. Remove the pan from the heat and stir in the shredded cheese until melted. Keep warm until ready to use.

2 Preheat the sandwich grill. Place the bread slices on a work surface and brush 1 side of each with the melted butter. Turn and spread the unbuttered sides with the mustard. On each of 2 of the bread slices, mustard sides up, layer one-fourth of the cheese, half of the ham, and half of the chives. Top with the remaining cheese on each. Place the remaining 2 bread slices on top, mustard sides down, and press to pack gently.

3 Place the panini in the grill, close the top plate, and cook until the bread is golden and toasted and the cheese is melted, 3–5 minutes. Meanwhile, preheat the broiler. Transfer the finished panini to a small baking sheet. Spoon the sauce over the sandwiches, then place under the broiler 3–4 inches from the heat source. Broil, watching carefully to prevent burning, until the sauce is bubbly and flecked with brown, about 1 minute. Transfer to plates and serve right away.

serves two

traditional cubano

This is the favorite sandwich of the Cuban communities in Tampa and Miami, served at snack bars called *loncherías*. Here, cilantro is added to update the classic combination of roasted pork, melted cheese, and pickles, but omit it if you want to be authentic.

1 Preheat the sandwich grill. Place the rolls, cut sides down, on a work surface and spread the crust sides with the butter. Turn and spread the cut sides with the mustard and sprinkle with the cilantro, if using. On each bottom half of the rolls, mustard sides up, layer one-fourth of the cheese, half of the pork, half of the ham, and 2 pickle slices. Top with the remaining cheese on each. Cover with the top halves of the rolls, mustard sides down, and press to pack gently.

2 Place the panini in the grill, close the top plate, and cook until the bread is golden and toasted, the cheese is melted, and the meats are warmed through, 3–5 minutes. Cut each sandwich in half and serve right away.

serves two

long Cuban rolls, Portuguese rolls, or submarine rolls, 2, split

unsalted butter, 1 tablespoon, at room temperature

Dijon mustard, 1 tablespoon

fresh cilantro, 1 tablespoon chopped (optional)

provolone cheese or Swiss cheese, 3 ounces, thinly sliced

roasted pork, 2 ounces, thinly sliced

Black Forest ham, 2 ounces, thinly sliced

thin dill pickle slices, 4

la plancha... The secret to this sandwich lies in the grilling and the traditional preparation requires the use of a grill similar to a panini maker. This trademark tool of Hispanic kitchens and cuisine is called *la plancha*.

sweet panini

strawberry shortcakes

Grilling the shortcakes updates this all-American dessert favorite made with fresh strawberries and rich whipped cream. You can also use grilled pound cake (page 84) if you don't have time to bake the shortcakes. You can substitute peaches or nectarines for the strawberries.

1 To make the shortcakes, preheat the oven to 400°F. Lightly grease a small baking sheet. In a food processor, combine the flour, sugar, baking powder, and salt and pulse to blend. Add the butter and pulse until the mixture has the texture of coarse meal. In a small bowl, whisk together the milk and egg yolk. With the motor running, add the milk mixture to the food processor and process just until dough comes together in clumps, about 5 seconds. Transfer the dough to a lightly floured work surface and knead 5–10 times to form a dough. Pat to about 1/2-inch thickness and use a cookie cutter to cut out four 3-inch rounds. Transfer to the baking sheet and bake until golden, 12–15 minutes. Transfer to a wire rack and let cool for at least 15 minutes or up to 2 hours.

2 In a bowl, using a fork, mash together half of the strawberries with 6 tablespoons of the sugar. Slice the remaining berries and add to the bowl. Let stand at room temperature for 20–30 minutes. In a bowl, combine the remaining 1 tablespoon sugar, the cinnamon, nutmeg, and cloves.

3 Preheat the sandwich grill. Split the shortcakes and brush on all sides with the melted butter. Sprinkle all over with the spiced sugar. Place in the grill, close the top plate, and cook until the shortcakes are lightly toasted and grill marked, 1–2 minutes; watch carefully to prevent burning.

4 Transfer 1 shortcake bottom to each of 4 small plates. Spoon the strawberries over the bottoms of the shortcakes, replace the tops, and garnish lavishly with dollops of whipped cream. Serve right away.

serves four

SHORTCAKES

all-purpose flour, 1 cup

sugar, 2 tablespoons

baking powder, 1 1/2 teaspoons

salt, 1/4 teaspoon

cold unsalted butter, 4 tablespoons, cut into small pieces

cold whole milk, 1/4 cup

egg yolk, 1

strawberries, 4 cups, hulled

sugar, 7 tablespoons

ground cinnamon, 1/4 teaspoon

grated nutmeg, 1/4 teaspoon

ground cloves, 1 pinch

unsalted butter, 1 tablespoon, melted

heavy cream, 1 cup, whipped to soft peaks, for serving

chocolate with raspberries & ricotta

Ruby raspberry jam, sweetened ricotta cheese, and rich, dark chocolate are a colorful and delicious combination. Any sweet yeast bread, such as challah or panettone, is a good choice. Garnish with chocolate and berries for a dramatic presentation.

whole-milk ricotta cheese, 1/3 cup

confectioners' sugar, 3 tablespoons

kirsch or other colorless fruit liqueur, 2 teaspoons

sweet challah bread or panettone, 4 slices, each about 1/2 inch thick

unsalted butter, 1 tablespoon, at room temperature

ground cinnamon, 1/4 teaspoon

raspberry jam, 1/4 cup

high-quality bittersweet chocolate, 3 ounces, chopped, plus chocolate curls for serving

fresh raspberries, 1/2 cup

1 Preheat the sandwich grill. In a bowl, stir together the ricotta, confectioners' sugar, and kirsch. Place the bread slices on a work surface and spread 1 side of each with the butter, then sprinkle with the cinnamon. Turn and spread the jam on 2 of the unbuttered sides, then carefully spread the ricotta mixture over the jam. Sprinkle with the chopped chocolate, then place the remaining 2 bread slices on top, jam sides down, and press to pack gently.

2 Place the panini in the grill, close the top plate, and cook until the bread is golden and toasted and the chocolate is melted. Carefully transfer to small plates and serve right away, garnished with the chocolate curls and raspberries.

serves two or four

[***working with chocolate...*** To make chocolate curls, first soften the chocolate bar by holding it in your hand for a minute or two. Then use a vegetable peeler to scrape delicate curls from the side of the softened chocolate bar.]

chocolate & hazelnut bananas

Italian-style chocolate-hazelnut spread can be found near the peanut butter in well-stocked grocery stores. Here, it is teamed with bananas and additional toasted hazelnuts. The combination of sweet, nutty, and fruity flavors makes an easy dessert or snack.

hazelnuts, 1/3 cup

sweet challah bread or panettone, 4 slices, each about 1/2 inch thick

chocolate-hazelnut spread, 1/4 cup

ripe but firm banana, 1, sliced

Frangelico or other hazelnut liqueur, 2 teaspoons (optional)

1 Place the hazelnuts in a small, dry skillet over medium-low heat. Cook, stirring constantly, until lightly toasted and fragrant, 5–7 minutes. Wrap the warm nuts completely in a clean kitchen towel and rub vigorously to remove the papery skins. Chop the nuts coarsely and set aside.

2 Preheat the sandwich grill. Place the bread slices on a work surface and spread 1 side of each with chocolate-hazelnut spread, then layer the banana on 2 of the slices. Drizzle the bananas with the liqueur, if using, then sprinkle with the chopped hazelnuts. Place the remaining 2 bread slices on top, spread sides down, and press to pack gently.

3 Place the panini in the grill, close the top plate, and cook until the bread is golden and toasted, the chocolate-hazelnut spread is melted, and the banana is warmed through, 2–4 minutes. Cut each sandwich in half and serve right away.

serves two

cinnamon-apple stuffed pancakes

The sandwich grill is a great way to utilize the extra pancakes from Sunday breakfast. Any buttermilk or sweet milk pancake is delicious here. This versatile preparation is a great dessert or the perfect centerpiece for a weekend lunch or brunch.

1 In a small bowl, stir together the sugar and cinnamon. Reserve 2 teaspoons of the mixture. In a frying pan, melt 2 tablespoons of the butter over medium heat. Add the cinnamon-sugar and the apples and sauté until the apples begin to soften, 2–3 minutes. Continue to cook, stirring often, until the cinnamon-sugar darkens and is caramelized and the apples are tender, 4–5 minutes. Stir in the Calvados and 2 tablespoons of the maple syrup and continue to cook for 1 minute longer. Keep warm until ready to use. (Alternatively, let cool, cover, and refrigerate for up to 4 hours. Reheat gently before serving.)

2 Preheat the sandwich grill. Melt the remaining 1 tablespoon butter in a small saucepan over medium-high heat. Place the pancakes on a work surface, brush 1 side of each with the melted butter, and sprinkle with the reserved cinnamon-sugar. Turn 2 of the pancakes buttered sides down and spread the unbuttered sides with the mascarpone. Place the remaining 2 pancakes on top, buttered sides up, and press to pack gently.

3 Place the panini in the grill, close the top plate, and cook until the pancakes are lightly toasted and grill marked and mascarpone is softened and warm, 1–2 minutes. Transfer to small plates, drizzle with the remaining 2 tablespoons maple syrup, and serve right away, with the cinnamon-apple mixture spooned over the top.

serves two

sugar, 1/4 cup

ground cinnamon, 1 1/4 teaspoons

unsalted butter, 3 tablespoons

Granny Smith apples, 2, peeled, cored, and thinly sliced

Calvados or apple cider, 2 tablespoons

pure maple syrup, 4 tablespoons

buttermilk pancakes, 4, cooked, each about 4 inches in diameter

mascarpone cheese, 4 tablespoons, at room temperature

honey-drizzled pears with gorgonzola & walnuts

This sophisticated, simple dessert relies on using ingredients of exceptional quality. Use lush, ripe pears, pure, fragrant honey, and the best Italian panettone you can find. It makes a great impression even when you have little time—it takes only 15 minutes to prepare.

walnuts, 3 tablespoons

sambuca or other anise liqueur, 2 tablespoons

pure herb honey or flower honey, $1\frac{1}{2}$ tablespoons

fresh lemon juice, 2 teaspoons

lemon zest, $\frac{1}{2}$ teaspoon grated

panettone, 2 slices, each about $\frac{1}{2}$ inch thick

walnut oil, 2 teaspoons

Gorgonzola cheese, $\frac{1}{4}$ cup, crumbled

small ripe but firm pears, 2, peeled, cored, and sliced

1 Place the walnuts in a small, dry skillet over medium-low heat. Cook, stirring constantly, until lightly toasted and fragrant, 5–7 minutes. Transfer right away to a cutting board to cool, then chop coarsely. Set aside.

2 In a small dish, stir together the sambuca, honey, and lemon juice and zest. Set aside.

3 Preheat the sandwich grill. Place the panettone slices on a work surface and brush on both sides with the walnut oil. Place in the grill, close the top plate, and cook until lightly toasted, 1–2 minutes.

4 Place 1 panettone slice on each of 2 small plates. Sprinkle the warm bread with half of the cheese. Arrange the sliced pears over and around the panettone, then drizzle with the honey mixture. Sprinkle with the remaining cheese and the toasted walnuts. Serve right away.

serves two

peach melba

This dessert is named after a famous Australian opera diva who enjoyed the combination of peaches and raspberries, a classic summer pairing. Use frozen raspberries for the sauce since they are more reliably ripe, but add fresh berries for a garnish, if you like.

frozen raspberries (not in syrup), one 10-ounce package, thawed

sugar, 6 tablespoons

seedless raspberry jam, 2 tablespoons

framboise or other raspberry liqueur, or raspberry syrup, 2 tablespoons

ripe peaches, 2, peeled, pitted, and sliced

fresh lemon juice, 2 teaspoons

pound cake, 2 slices, each about 1/2 inch thick, or 2 shortcakes (page 77) or biscuits, split

unsalted butter, 1 tablespoon, melted

grated nutmeg, 1/4 teaspoon

whipped cream or pistachio ice cream for serving

fresh raspberries for garnish (optional)

1 Put the thawed frozen raspberries in a food processor and process to a purée. Strain the purée through a fine-mesh sieve into a bowl, pressing on the seeds and solids with the back of a spoon to extract as much liquid as possible. Discard the contents of the sieve. Add 3 tablespoons of the sugar, the jam, and the liqueur to the purée and let stand, stirring occasionally, until the sugar dissolves, 5–10 minutes. In a small bowl, stir together the peaches, the remaining 3 tablespoons sugar, and the lemon juice. Let stand, stirring often, until sugar is dissolved and the peaches become somewhat juicy, 5–10 minutes. (The peaches and raspberry sauce can be prepared up to 3 hours ahead, covered, and refrigerated. Return to room temperature before serving.)

2 Preheat the sandwich grill. Place the pound cake on a work surface, brush on both sides with the melted butter, and sprinkle all over with the nutmeg. Place in the grill, close the top plate, and cook until pale golden and grill marked, 2–3 minutes.

3 Divide the cake between 2 small plates. Spoon the peaches over the cake, then ladle the raspberry sauce over and around the peaches and cake. Serve right away with a dollop with whipped cream, garnished with fresh berries, if you like.

serves two

grilled pineapples on coconut pound cake

Pineapple takes particularly well to grilling, and not just because it is sturdy. On the grill, the fruit's natural sugars caramelize, deepening its flavor, color, and texture. Homemade pound cake is best, but a high-quality purchased pound cake works as well.

1 Place the macadamia nuts in a small, dry skillet over medium-low heat. Cook, stirring constantly, until lightly toasted and fragrant, 5–7 minutes. Transfer immediately to a cutting board to cool, then chop coarsely. Set aside.

2 Preheat a sandwich grill. Brush both sides of the pineapple slices with the melted butter, then sprinkle all over with the brown sugar, patting to help it adhere. Arrange the pineapple in the grill, close the top plate, and cook until grill marked and the sugar darkens and begins to caramelize, 1–2 minutes. Transfer to a plate. Place the pound cake slices on a work surface and sprinkle on both sides with the allspice. Place in the grill, close the top, and cook until pale golden and grill marked, 1–2 minutes, watching carefully to prevent burning.

3 Place 1 pound cake slice on each of 2 small plates. Cut the pineapple slices in half crosswise and arrange over the pound cake. Drizzle with the rum and sprinkle with the toasted nuts. Serve right away with the ice cream, if desired.

serves two

macadamia nuts, 1/3 cup

fresh pineapple, 2 large slices, each about 1/2 inch thick

unsalted butter, 1 tablespoon, melted

light brown sugar, 2 tablespoons

firm coconut pound cake or regular pound cake, 2 slices, each about 1/2 inch thick

allspice, 1/2 teaspoon

dark rum, 2 tablespoons

coconut ice cream for serving (optional)

companion recipes

homemade potato chips

russet potatoes, 2, unpeeled

peanut oil for frying

salt and freshly ground pepper

Using a mandoline or a sharp knife, slice the potatoes as thinly as possible. Place the slices in a large bowl and add ice water to cover. Let stand for about 1 hour then drain well and transfer to paper towels until they are very dry.

Fill a large, heavy saucepan halfway with oil and heat until a deep-frying thermometer reads 325°F. Add the potato slices in batches and fry until they look firm and just begin to crisp around the edges, 2–3 minutes.

Using a slotted spoon, carefully transfer the potatoes to paper towels to drain. When all the potatoes have been fried once, let them cool for 15 minutes. Meanwhile, heat the oil until until a deep-frying thermometer reads 375°F.

In batches, fry the potatoes a second time, until they are crisp and dark golden brown, another 1–2 minutes.

Using a slotted spoon, transfer the finished potato chips to paper towels to drain. Sprinkle with salt and pepper to taste and serve at once. (Store any leftover potato chips tightly covered at room temperature for up to 1 week.)

serves two

sweet potato wedges

sweet potatoes, 2, unpeeled

extra-virgin olive oil, 1/4 cup, plus more for greasing

fresh oregano or rosemary, 2 teaspoons chopped

red pepper flakes, pinch (optional)

salt and freshly ground pepper

Preheat the oven to 500°F and grease a rimmed baking sheet with olive oil.

Cut the potatoes lengthwise into thick wedges and place them in a bowl. Pour the 1/4 cup olive oil over the top of the potatoes and sprinkle with the chopped herbs, the red pepper flakes, if using, and salt and pepper to taste. Stir and toss to coat the potatoes evenly with the oil.

Place the potato wedges about 1 inch apart on the baking sheet and roast, turning once, for about 20 minutes, until tender when pierced with a fork. Transfer to paper towels to drain briefly then serve.

Variation: Substitute Russet potatoes or yams for the sweet potatoes.

serves two

shoestring fries

russet potatoes, 2, peeled, cut into 1/8-inch slices

canola oil for frying

salt and freshly ground pepper

flat-leaf parsley, 1/2 cup chopped

Cut the potato slices lengthwise into thin strips about 1/8 inch wide.

Fill a large, heavy saucepan halfway with oil and heat until a deep-frying thermometer reads 375°F. Add the potato strips in batches and fry until golden brown, 2–3 minutes.

Transfer the potato strips to paper towels to drain, allow them to cool briefly, then serve, sprinkled with the salt, pepper, and chopped parsley.

serves two

aioli

large fresh egg, 1, at room temperature

fresh lemon juice, 1 tablespoon

Dijon mustard, 1 teaspoon

canola oil, 3/4 cup

extra-virgin olive oil, 3/4 cup

garlic cloves, 3, minced

salt and freshly ground pepper

Crack the egg into a food processor and add the lemon juice and mustard. Mix the oils together in a glass measuring cup.

With the processor running, very slowly add the mixed oils in a steady stream. Process until the mixture thickens, emulsifies, and turns opaque in color, occasionally stopping the processor to scrape down the sides with a rubber spatula, 1 1/2–2 minutes. Add the garlic and process to combine.

Transfer the aioli to a dish and season to taste with salt and pepper. (Store tightly covered in the refrigerator for up to 5 days.)

makes two cups

fresh tomato salsa

jalapeño, 1

plum tomatoes, 3, seeded and diced

white onion, 1/4 cup finely diced

fresh cilantro, 2 teaspoons minced (optional)

fresh lime juice, 1 teaspoon

garlic clove, 1, minced

salt and freshly ground pepper

Cut the jalapeño lengthwise into quarters and use the tip of the knife to cut out the stem, ribs, and seeds; reserve the ribs and seeds. Cut the quarters into strips, then mince the strips.

In a bowl, combine the minced jalapeño, tomato, onion, cilantro (if using), lime juice, and garlic. Season to taste with salt and pepper and let stand at room temperature for 15 minutes to allow the flavors to blend.

Mince the jalapeño ribs and add the seeds and ribs to adjust the heat to your taste. (Store tightly covered in the refrigerator for up to 12 hours.)

makes two cups

glossary

Apple butter With a consistency like butter, this tart fruit spread or condiment is a concentrated form of applesauce. It can be found in specialty food stores.

Balsamic vinegar Made from unfermented grape juice, balsamic vinegar may be aged from 1 to 75 years. Top quality, aged balsamic is sold at specialty-food stores, but inexpensive versions can be found at most supermarkets.

Bread, Artisan Handcrafted and made with the highest-quality ingredients, artisan bread can be found in a variety of styles and shapes. Many artisan bakeries have their own specialty breads, like olive, walnut, crusty country-style, or sourdough.

Bread, Challah A high-rising, egg-rich yeast bread that is served at traditional Jewish holidays. The bread may be formed into elaborate loaves.

Bread, Cuban rolls Similar to French bread but with lard added to the dough, Cuban bread is heavier and less prone to drying out. You can substitute French bread rolls or Kaiser rolls.

Bread, Focaccia Yeast dough that is flattened, stretched, and dimpled before baking so that the finished loaf has a bumpy surface.

Bread, Portuguese Made with milk, sugar or honey, this bread is sweet and light in texture. It is often served toasted with butter or for dessert. You can find this bread at Portuguese bakeries or through online sources.

Bread, Semolina Semolina is a gritty, golden flour milled from high-protein durum wheat. It is often used in dried pasta, pizza dough, and other breads. Look for it at a health-food or specialty food store.

Calvados This dry apple brandy aged in oak comes from northern France, where apples are plentiful. It is widely available at liquor stores.

Capicola This prized Italian cured meat can be found in Italian delicatessens or other specialty food stores. You can substitute other, more widely available cured meats like salami or prosciutto.

Cheese, Boursin A creamy cow's milk cheese flavored with herbs or garlic, or both, this soft, easy-to-spread cheese is available at most supermarkets.

Cheese, Fontina A mild, fruity Italian cow's milk cheese with a pleasing firmness and light but heady aroma.

Cheese, Gorgonzola An exceptional cow's milk blue cheese from Italy with a moist, creamy texture and complex flavor.

Cheese, Manchego A Spanish sheep's milk cheese with a pale yellow interior dotted with holes and a slightly salty flavor.

Cheese, Marscarpone A very soft, rich, smooth, fresh Italian cheese made from cream, with a texture reminiscent of sour cream.

Chiles, chipotle These are jalapeño chiles that have been dried with smoky heat. They are often sold in a powder form, but they can also be found canned in a spicy chile sauce called adobo.

Chorizo Chorizo is a pork sausage that is seasoned with garlic and paprika. Spanish chorizo may be fresh, cured, dried, or smoked, but it always has a slightly tangy flavor. Mexican chorizo is an assertively spicy fresh sausage.

Cornichons Also called gherkins, these small, sour pickles have a tart flavor and crisp texture.

Five-spice powder This potent spice usually contains cloves, aniseeds or fennel seeds, star anise, cinnamon, Sichuan peppercorns, and ginger.

Framboise A type of fruit brandy, framboise is a strong, clear spirit distilled from fermented raspberry juice. It is served before or after dinner and is widely used in desserts.

Ginger, pickled Familiar to anyone who loves sushi, pickled ginger is used in Japan as a palate cleanser. It is available in Asian specialty-food markets.

Greens, turnip These greens are found attached to baby turnips and are extremely healthful—high in vitamins, K, A, and C. Look for greens that are unblemished, crisp, and deep green in color.

Ham, Black Forest This prized version of smoked ham is from the Black Forest region in Germany and is flavored with garlic, coriander, pepper, and juniper berries. It can be found at specialty food stores.

Kirsch A cherry-flavored colorless brandy, the best of which is made in Germany, France, and Switzerland, where the wild black cherry is used.

Mortadella This type of salami is made with ground pork, at least 15% pork fat, and is flavored with black pepper, myrtle berries, nutmeg, coriander, and sometimes has pistachio nuts.

New-England cut hot dog buns These buns, unique to New England, are top-sliced and have flat sides. They are often buttered, grilled, and filled with hot dogs or used to make lobster rolls.

Panettone This labor-intensive bread is made for Christmas all over Italy, but can be found at specialty food stores or online in the United States. It is flavored with raisins and other candied fruits or nuts.

Paprika, smoked This Spanish version is made from ground dried red peppers and is available as sweet, half-sweet, or hot. Sweet paprika is often specified in recipes.

Pepper, Poblano Large and fairly mild, the fresh dark green poblano is about 5 inches (13 cm) long and has broad "shoulders." Poblanos have a nutty flavor and are often stuffed for chile rellenos.

Sambuca This Italian, anise-flavored liqueur is infused with witch elder bush and licorice, and sweetened with sugar.

Tapenade Capers, anchovies, and garlic are some of the other ingredients that go into this classic Provençal olive spread.

Tomatoes, sun-dried Fresh tomatoes dried in the sun take on a deep, intense tomato flavor and chewy, dense texture. You can find them packed in oil at specialty-food stores.

Tuna, Ahi "Ahi" is the Hawaiian name for Yellowfin tuna, which can reach a weight of 300 pounds. A prized food fish, the tuna comes from a family of large fish with rich, oily, firm flesh.

Wasabi powder Wasabi is a root that is most often found grated into a paste and served alongside sushi. The powder form can be found in specialty food stores and can be mixed with water to create a paste or sauce.

index

D

E

F

G

H

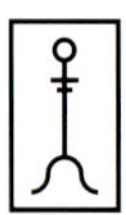

FIRESIDE
A Division of Simon & Schuster, Inc.
1230 Avenue of the Americas
New York, NY 10020

WELDON OWEN INC.

Chief Executive Officer, Weldon Owen Group John Owen
President and Chief Executive Officer, Weldon Owen Inc. Terry Newell
Vice President, International Sales Stuart Laurence
Vice President, Sales & New Business Development Amy Kaneko
Vice President & Creative Director Gaye Allen
Vice President & Publisher Hannah Rahill
Director of Finance Mark Perrigo
Executive Editor Jennifer Newens
Art Director Kara Church
Senior Designer Ashley Martinez
Production Director Chris Hemesath
Production Manager Michelle Duggan
Color Manager Teri Bell

ACKNOWLEDGMENTS

Photographers Lara Hata
Food Stylist Jennifer Straus
Prop Stylist Leigh Noe
Photographer's Assistants Heidi K. Ladendorf and Jennifer Hale
Assistant Food Stylist Alexa Hyman and Christine Wolheim
Copy Editor Sharon Silva
Proofreader Melissa Eatough
Indexer Ken DellaPenta

Originally published in August 2007 by Weldon Owen Inc.

First Fireside hardcover edition March 2009

Set in Avenir
Color separations by Embassy Graphics
Printed and Bound in China by Midas Printing
10 9 8 7 6 5 4 3 2 1

Library of Congress Cataloging-in-Publication data is available.

ISBN-13: 978-1-4391-0808-6
ISBN-10: 1-4391-0808-0